631ART.COM PRESENTS:
"BIRDS IN FLIGHT"
BY EDDIE ALFARO

BIRDS ARE A MIRACLE BECAUSE THEY PROVE TO
US THERE IS A FINER, SIMPLER STATE OF BEING
WHICH WE MAY STRIVE TO ATTAIN.
- DOUGLAS COUPLAND

HUMMINGBIRD

AN OWL IS THE WISEST OF ALL BIRDS BECAUSE
THE MORE IT SEES THE THE LESS IT TALKS.
- CHRISTIE WATSON

HAWKS ARE THE MOST KEEN-EYED AND EFFICIENT HUNTERS.

MAY YOU SOAR ON EAGLE WINGS, HIGH
ABOVE THE MADNESS OF THE WORLD.
- JONATHAN LOCKWOOD HUIE

THE TERM WATER BIRD, ALTERNATIVELY, WATERBIRD OR AQUATIC BIRD IS USED TO REFER TO BIRDS THAT LIVE ON OR AROUND WATER.

HEAR HOW THE BIRDS, ON EVERY BLOOMING SPRAY,
WITH JOYOUS MUSIC WAKE THE DAWNING DAY.
- ALEXANDER POPE

GULLS

OSPREY

OBSERVE AND REFLECT, AND BECOME
A LITTLE WISER EVERY DAY.

A VERY GREAT VISION IS NEEDED AND THE
MAN WHO HAS IT MUST FOLLOW IT AS THE
EAGLE SEEKS THE DEEPEST BLUE OF THE SKY.
- TA' SHUNKE WITKO

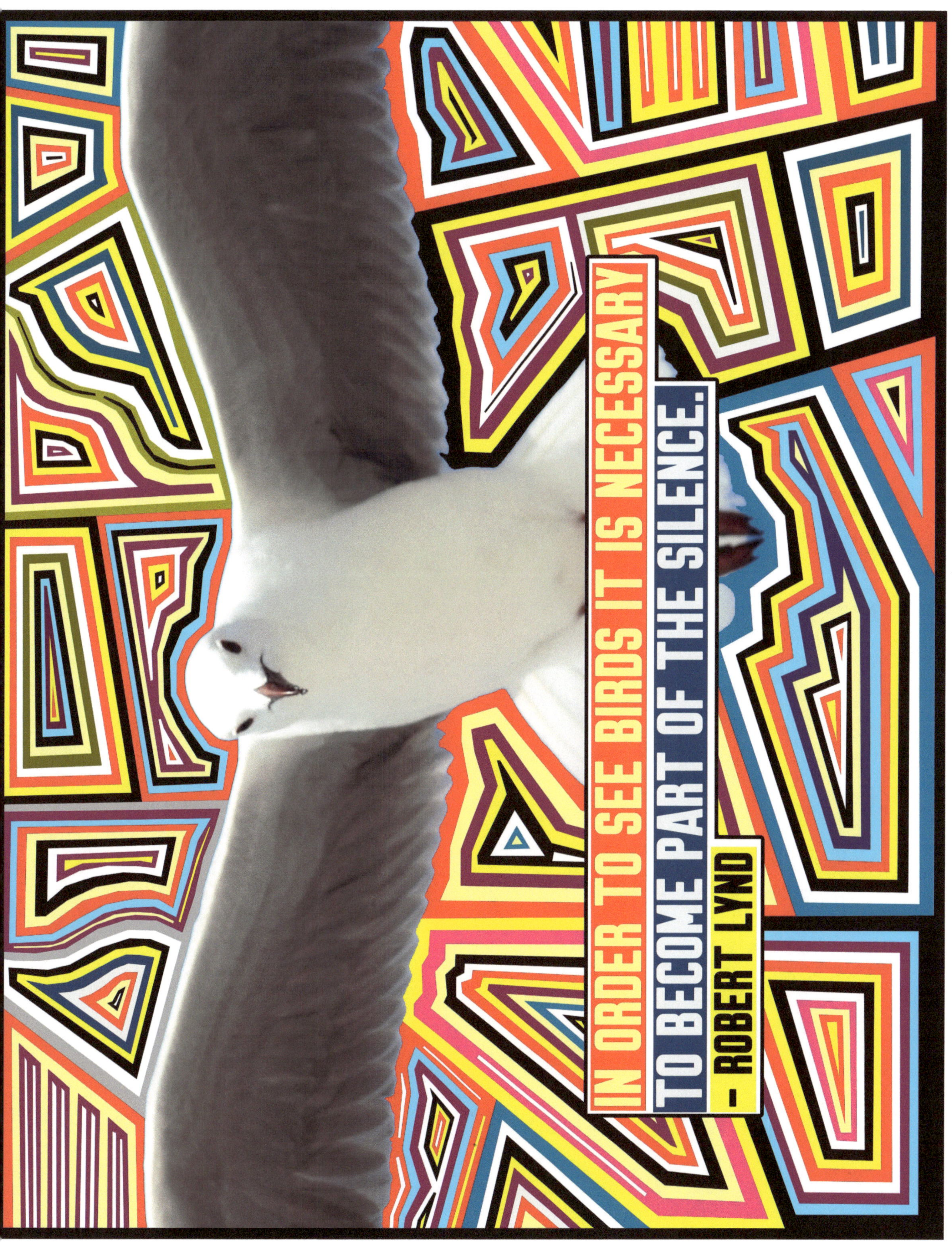

IN ORDER TO SEE BIRDS IT IS NECESSARY
TO BECOME PART OF THE SILENCE.
– ROBERT LYND

"BE LIKE THE BIRD THAT, PASSING ON HER FLIGHT AWHILE ON BOUGHS TOO SLIGHT, FEELS THEM GIVE WAY BENEATH HER, AND YET SINGS, KNOWING THAT SHE HATH WINGS." — VICTOR HUGO

FUN FACTS ABOUT BIRDS:

THE SWORD-BILLED HUMMINGBIRD IS THE ONLY BIRD WITH A BILL LONGER THAN ITS BODY.

THERE ARE OVER 9,500 SPECIES OF BIRDS IN THE WORLD.

APPROXIMATELY 2/3 OF ALL THE BIRD SPECIES ARE FOUND IN TROPICAL RAIN FORESTS.

OWLS CANNOT SWIVEL THEIR EYES. INSTEAD THEY MOVE THEIR HEADS COMPLETELY AROUND TO SEE STRAIGHT BEHIND THEM.

MANY BIRDS, SUCH AS STARLINGS, SING NOTES TOO HIGH FOR HUMANS TO HEAR.

A GREEN WOODPECKER CAN EAT AS MANY AS 2,000 ANTS PER DAY.

A PELICAN'S POUCH-LIKE BEAK CAN HOLD UP TO 2.5 GALLONS OF WATER AT A TIME.

THE BIRD THAT LAYS THE SMALLEST EGG IN THE WORLD IS THE BEE HUMMINGBIRD.

IN THE UNITED STATES ALONE, THERE ARE OVER 40 MILLION PET BIRDS.

A BIRD'S FEATHERS WEIGH MORE THAN ITS SKELETON.

THE BIRD WITH THE GREATEST WINGSPAN OF ANY OTHER BIRD IS THE WANDERING ALBATROSS AT UP TO 11.8 FT

THE FASTEST FLYING BIRD IN A DIVE IS THE PEREGRINE FALCON. IT AVERAGES SPEEDS OF OVER 110 MPH.

THE WORD "PARAKEET" LITERALLY MEANS "LONG TAIL."

IN THE NOVEL TO KILL A MOCKINGBIRD (1960), AUTHOR HARPER LEE USED THE MOCKINGBIRD TO SYMBOLIZE INNOCENCE.

A BALD EAGLE IS CALLED "BALD" BECAUSE IT IS PIEBALD (BLACK AND WHITE), NOT BECAUSE IT DOESN'T HAVE ANY FEATHERS.

AN ALBATROSS CAN SOAR FOR AS LONG AS SIX HOURS WITHOUT MOVING ITS WINGS.

THERE ARE MORE FAKE FLAMINGOS ON EARTH THAN REAL ONES.

A FLOCK OF RAVENS IS CALLED AN "UNKINDNESS" OR A "CONSPIRACY."

THANK YOU.
THE END.

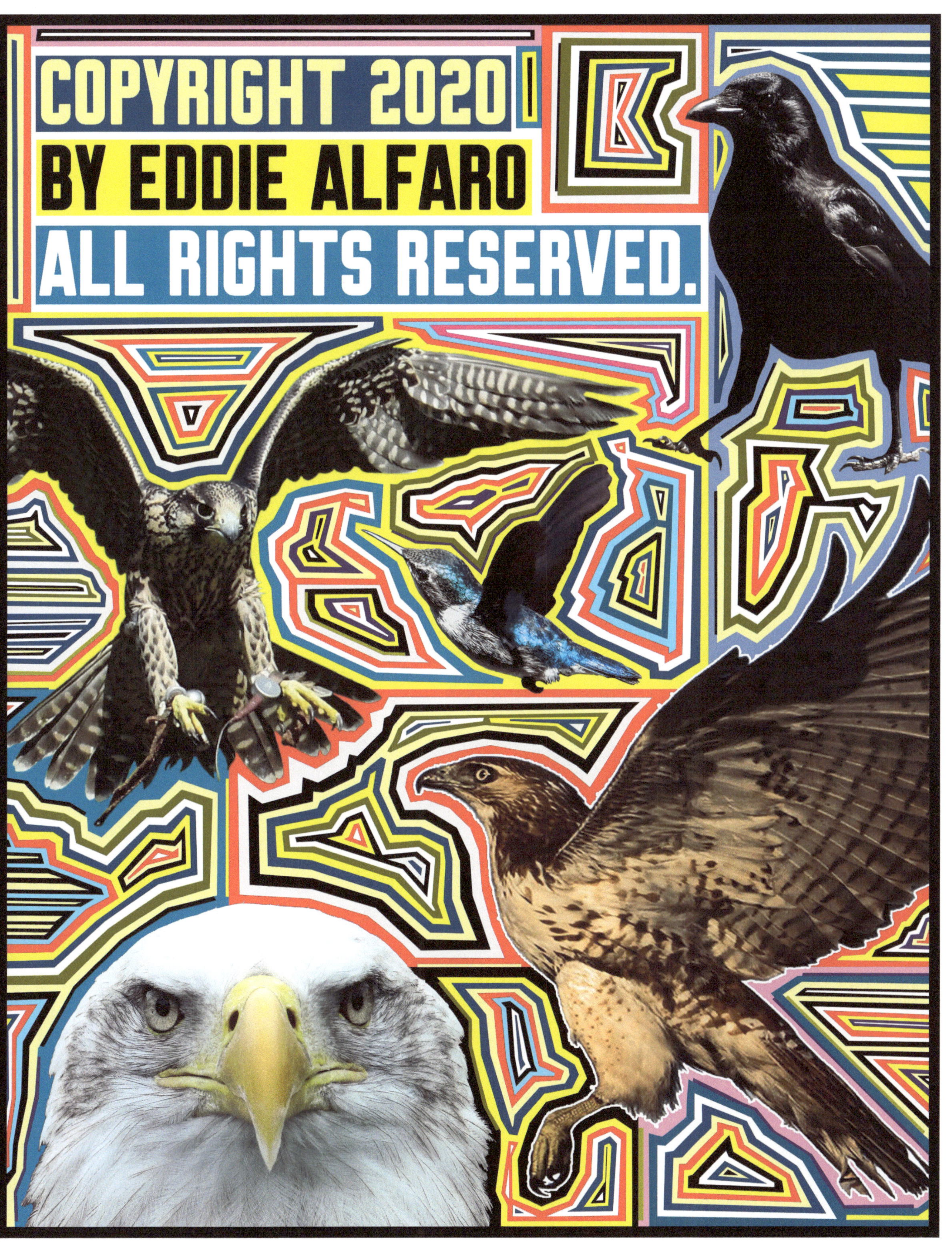
COPYRIGHT 2020
BY EDDIE ALFARO
ALL RIGHTS RESERVED.

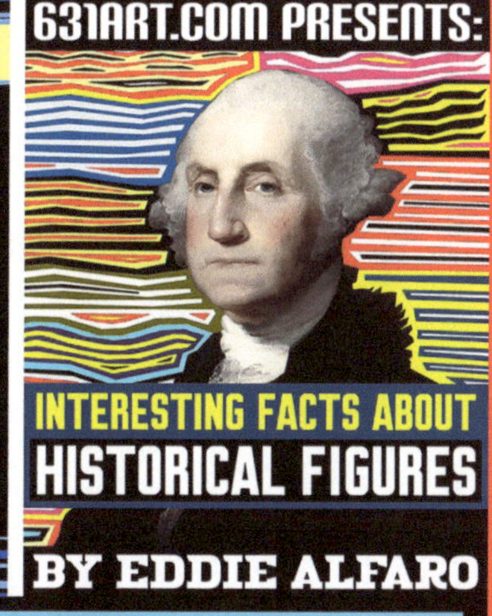

MORE BOOKS AT:

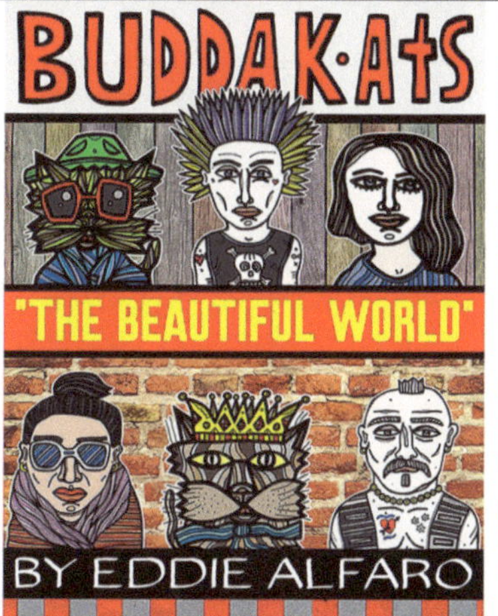

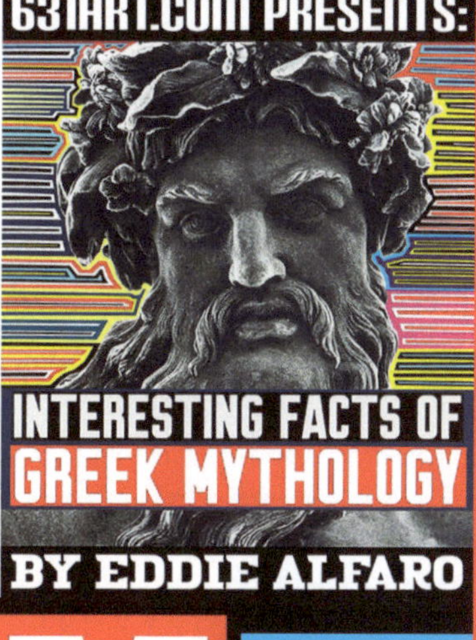

631ART.COM

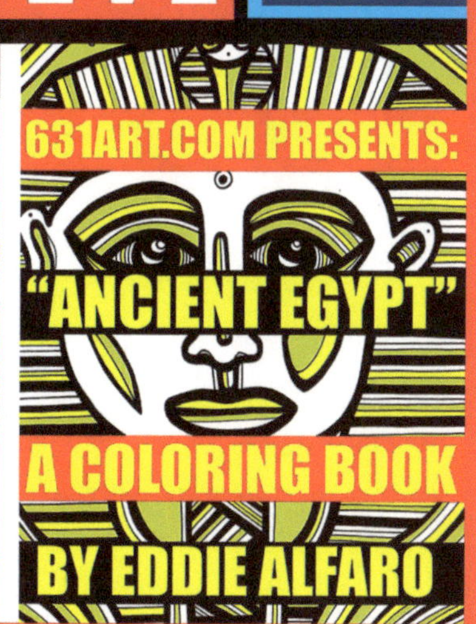

www.ingramcontent.com/pod-product-compliance
Lightning Source LLC
Chambersburg PA
CBHW040139240726
48664CB00002B/539